M. D. Shafrir-Stillman

Interpretations

Biblical Verses & Meditative Poems

M. D. Shafrir-Stillman

Interpretations

Biblical Verses & Meditative Poems

Senior Editors & Producers: Contento

Translators: S.R., Yona Mashmoor, Dov Shneorson, Ruth Tennenbaum, Karen Alkalay-Gut.

Cover Photo and Design: Zvika Zelikovich

Book Design: Liliya Lev Ari

ISBN: 978-965-550-484-2

International sole distributor: Contento
22 Isserles Street, 6701457, Tel Aviv, Israel
www.ContentoNow.com
Netanel@contento-publishing.com

M. D. Shafrir-Stillman

Interpretations

Biblical Verses & Meditative Poems

CONTENTO**NOW**

For my beloved family

Table of Contents:

Poems on Life, Love and Death

Introductory Poems

Who Is the Poet?

You may not know it, but the poet
Must be a sort of diver,
Diving into the depths of the soul,
Trying to expose the corals of feeling amid the shoal.

He may not show it, but a poet
Is a man who has the urge and the passion to be heard
Till his voice echoes and flies like a bird
And merges to be one with the spirit of his fellow man.

But I think that the writing of a poet
Is created simply because –
Without it he cannot doze,
As it makes him immerse in his thoughts
And not leave them and collapse
In a frenetic dance till he loses his senses
Or flies high, like Icarus,
Rises sky high-
Melted, dissolves in the heat of the sun,
Or leaps out of his mind, running like a fool
Into the vale of tears of the soul.

The Destiny of the Poem

"Come up with me into my lot...and I likewise will go with thee into thy lot."

THE BOOK OF JUDGES (CHAPTER 1:3)

To be written on the ice,
To be melted from solid state to water,
To be evaporated in the turbulent wind,
To be read in the shapes of the clouds,
To be heard surprisingly by the rain,
To be merged in the roots of the grass,
To be drained to the stream of the river,
To be dissolved among the waves of the ocean, or
To be permeated into the ground water of oblivion.
And if indeed this is the destiny of my poem
Then I will say directly to him:
I likewise will go with you into your lot.

What is a True Poem?

Although some say that the best poem is deception,
I wish to write an authentic poem.
Will this poem actually be so?
And if it is a true and honest thing,
- How will we know?
I have another question, I must admit:
If it really is thoroughly true
Which truth is it?

Is this preferable truth?
One that must
Exist in this poem,
As it flows pleasantly,
Moderately and sensibly,
Or must this poem
Be born out of a storm of emotions
And gales in the depths of the soul?

And though I write the poem on a computer
- I don't trust it, and I rewrite it later,
Since I write it at night,
When I'm really drunk with words
And I get up the next morning with a hangover,
And I suffer all day, feeling drowsy and confused,

And if I write it by hand,
On pure white paper, am I to understand
That everything written in ink
Is actually where the truth begins?
And does it correctly convey
The truth anyway?

The World between Its Reality and Its Appearance

Not so, it is not actually so,
As each person differs from his brother
- Even though it seems to be so,
Even if they appear to be alike.

And thus the eyes are blocked and could not see,
And the minds are blocked from observing.
The real world is not so
Even though it seems so.

For between the real world
And the world of false impressions,
There is a chasm which will never
Be bridged over the waters.

And there is still darkness over the waters of the deep,
And the Spirit of God still moves upon the face of the waters.

Poetry Celebrates

(Written after the battle against Hammas in the Gaza strip - Summer 2014)

The cannons fire and poetry is silent.
All the waves are high, the storm continues.
All the flags are taken down, the war is over.

The soldiers all return to their worried families.
And those badly wounded – their healing continues.
All our feelings rise for a longed-for healing.

All the seagulls fly and the fish are frightened.
All the dogs bark at a passing procession,
But the procession passes and poetry celebrates.

Biblical Verses

The Creation of the World and of Man

(Poem for Yom Kippur, Day of Atonement)

In the beginning, God created
The heavens and the earth.
And then he created the rest by proclamation:
The first thing to be created was the light of day,
Which was differentiated from the darkness;
The second thing was the firmament, which then became a sky,
Which separated waters from waters;
The third thing to be created by proclamation was the land,
Which appeared from the same waters.
And so on and so forth did our great
Lord continue to create...
Thus, the creator made more things in His universe,
All created out of chaos
(Meaning lack of form or order
In some wilderness or emptiness)
And from this disorder in the universe
He created and made some order.

And if all things in the world
Were created by proclamation of God,
It is only man that He made
In His image, in His likeness,
As humans are superior to all other animals.

And if this is the way God made man,
Without many words spoken,
His representative he would become,
To rule over the animals in His kingdom,
To till His soil, ploughing and planting,
And to cultivate the vegetation for a living;
Why did God not also make him
A man of morals who would never sin?

Secular thoughts on the first
2 verses of the Bible

A. *"In the beginning God created the heaven and the earth."*

(GENESIS 1:1)

... And the earth was astonished:
What had happened to the heaven?
As although he had already known
About their appointment
He hadn't come to meet her,
As had been decided earlier,
On the line of the horizon?

B. *"And the earth was without form and void. And darkness*
was upon the deep. And the Spirit of God moved upon the
face of the waters."

(GENESIS 1:2)

I. He, who created
All the universe,
Apologizes deeply
For this dark situation
That happened because
He simply took time out
For thought of re-evaluation.

2. Maybe because God was everywhere in its own creation
   And was tired of making the earth and heaven,
   He decided that His spirit
   Is to be evaporated from its waters.

The First Man Asks

Suddenly I came into the world,
Just like that - I came without my consent
And thus, all of a sudden, I was in the world,
A mature man, deprived of a childhood
Created in the image of God
(Without being asked).
- To have dominion over all animals
And to be fruitful and multiply
And fill the world with human beings.

Now I already know:
Sometime I will also leave
This world.
No one will ask me
When, what and how my end will be.
Therefore, every time, without permission
Like a child, I examine
What am I to myself?
(I know not for certain).
Who am I to myself?
(I myself do not realize).
How am I to myself?
(I do not recognize).

And thus I always ask
But God gives me no answer,
- Therefore I am not for myself
And there is no one for me.

Madam, I'm Adam

"Madam, I'm Adam,"
Said Adam to Eve,
To the unashamed naked first woman on earth,
On the eve of humanity,
On the eve of great events.

"Madam, I'm Adam
And you are my woman Eve, made by the Lord.
And you are created to be my helper,
To be my wife and one flesh with me,
So try to make the best of it."

"But Madam, is it that we had no childhood
That something would be wrong and evil
In our or in our offspring's deeds,
That God would repent that he had made us
And would create another sort of mankind?"

"Oh Adam, my Adam",
Answered Eve, the mother of all living humans,
"When our eyes of adults created without boyhood
Will be opened wide to see and know
What we are and how we are,
- Let's try to be all the time of our lives
As naked and pure as just-born babies,
Then we shall be virtuous people
And do no evil forever."

Knowing Good and Evil

He was a simple man
And was not very clever,
Tough in the image of God he was created
(To be a grown man without childhood).
But after what happened
A long time ago
In the Garden of Eden
- He should have already known
What is good and what is evil.

A simple man he was,
A person knowing more or less
(Much less than more)
What is good and what is evil.
So, maybe we should pray to the Creator:
Let it be that his human creature
Observes much better
The Difference
Between good and evil.

God – I Do Not Understand

God – I do not understand the order of creation:
How is it you created, in sequence and by proclamation
The land and vegetation on the third day
(on the third day "it was good" appears twice),
But You only created the sources of light, including the sun,
the next day,
While plants cannot live or be without sun,
(While chlorophyll feeds them, and with it they produce all three
Of the major food groups, which give life to all beings)?

God – I still do not understand Your ways:
How is it that the whole world was created
in six days (by proclamation),
And after animals were created on the land, on the sixth day,
Only then did You create the first man last (and by action),
And in your kindness you also gave him a very long time to live,
Of no less than nine hundred and thirty years?

God – I also do not understand the meaning of Your ways:
For example, how did Enoch rise to heaven,
After living for three hundred and sixty five years?
And if he did become an angel, what is his role
And what does he do in the skies, both then and nowadays?
What happens to the other angels?
Do they still go up and down a ladder, as they did once?

How are the sons of God, the giants,
After between them and the daughters of Eve
Blossomed romance?
By the way, who was Noah's wife, and what was her name?
The second mother of humanity, the one after Our Mother Eve?
(It is unlikely that she was Na'ama, daughter of Zilla, sixth
generation of Cain's dynasty, whilst Noah was of the eighth
generation of Seth; thus, Na'ama was old already, the age of
his grandmother, wife of Methuselah).

God – I have asked about several chapters in the book of Genesis,
About the creation,
But I still have many questions.
And after a long time, some seventy years,
I am still patient, waiting and hoping to know for certain
Especially about the question:
Why is the suffering of your chosen people so great,
Children of Eber, Noah's grandson of
his great-grandson,
Both when they were far away in exile and now,
After they have returned to their homeland?

Farewell, Everyone

a.

Farewell, Adam.
Some say that before you were created
God convened the council of angels
And it was finally decided,
Not by a large majority,
That you would be created
And the decision was recorded:
"Let us make man in our image, after our likeness".
Although the minority expected
That you would always carry a 'sack of sins',
Versus the majority who hoped
You would be a loyal messenger and a wonder of creation,
Who safeguards all creatures and plants in Eden.
Therefore, you were created last, on the final day of creation,
After all the others created in the world,
Who may have prepared the whole world for your coming
And your enjoyment, on condition that you would not sin,
Otherwise, you would work hard for a living.

And if you should have some good days,
They would only be specks of good,
Since, most of the time you will feel bad
And not just a tad.

b.

"Hello Madam
I'm Adam
And you shall be named woman,
For you were taken from a man,
And I am the man
And you were taken from me.
You are a bone of my bones
One of my ribs
- Wrapped with flesh from my flesh,
For we became one
After feasting on the fruit of the forbidden tree.

Farewell Madam Eve
I loved you naked
And I love you dressed
With a fig leaf and a belt.
"Be fruitful and multiply," our creator ordered
And who are we to defy his word,
As He is the supreme lord
And we are, in comparison, like the grass in the field.

Eve Our Mother

And again I return to her, to Eve.
Eve from Genesis, Our Mother Eve;
And again, I wish to know:
Did Eve actually sin
Or did she rebel and
Shake off responsibility?
For she broke the strict prohibition,
By eating from the forbidden fruit,
Or perhaps she preferred to know
What good and bad were
To a life in Eden, eternal life
Which lingers forever, tiresomely,
Without joys or grief
Deeds or activity.

And thus Eve set humanity free
And released all from their naiveté
Towards a life of meaning and actuality,
To a way of life of emotion and spirit
Wisdom and knowledge,
Which has a start, a middle and an end, when they die
After they guide their offspring how to continue with life.

About the Serpent

"And the serpent was more subtle than any beast of the field"
Maybe because it was the first one
To eat from the fruit (though it was never vegetarian)
Which chose to know what bad is, only bad,
And did not learn at all about the good in the world;
And perhaps that is why it wanted, in all its cunning,
To be *"an help meet"* for Adam, instead of his wife.

And wise men have said that the serpent
Was also called *'angel serpent'*,
Before it was cursed,
That it had ears, limbs and wings
Walked the earth and flew up to the skies.
And that it also had a sense of a foreseeing snake
-*"Ye shall not surely die"*, said the snake
Who could speak, so he whispered to Eve,
Who feared to eat from the forbidden fruit,
But she, as we know, could not resist temptation
And ate of the fruit
For she could not overcome her sin.

Or perhaps the *'angel serpent'*
Promised her eternal youth:
"Look how pretty you will be, just like me
After I shed my skin and lost my wrinkles."

But the subtil serpent didn't foresee his future correctly,
Nor God's curse on him:
"thou art cursed...upon thy belly shalt thou go,
and dust shalt thou eat all the days of thy life."
But maybe the serpent consoled itself
By the fact that Adam, created from dust – shall end in dust.

The Serpent's Skin

"It does not bother me at all",
Said the old serpent,
"If it was said that I am a cunning beast,
If I was determined to be cursed
More than any other animal of the field
That the Lord God had made."

"I don't care at all",
Said the aged serpent,
If I crawl upon my belly on the ground
And if I eat dust all my life.
Because what is essential to me is to remove
My old hide, only to cast away my skin."

"What is the Lord God to me?
And who is Eve for me
If my old hide remains on me
And is pressing me till I can't anymore
Contain it in my body
Which is growing and crawling all the time."

The Voice That Was Walking About

*"And they heard the voice of the Lord God walking in the garden
in the cool of the day: and Adam and his wife hid themselves..."*
(GENESIS 3:8)

And the two of them,
Who hid among the branches of the apple tree,
Heard the voice well, walking through the trees in Eden
Though it was a searching voice
And may have spoken anxiously and firmly.
And they two, who already knew
Each other, as well as good from bad
(And though they were nude,
They were not ashamed, nor did they feel guilty or sad),
They must have been amazed:
The voice could have run or flown in the wind,
Developing speed of eight hundred miles per hour;
But without the speaker's image –
His voice was so terrible and stormy,
And even cast fear, like great thunder on a cloudless day;
And the spirit of God,
Which always moved silently
Suddenly blew from the face of the waters
At such speed
That it turned their daylight
Into darkness upon the face of the deep.

Expelled from the Garden of Eden

Ever since they were hastily expelled from the Garden,
And with the heat of the flaming sword –
And just like we left the warm, comfortable womb –
Through the birth canal,
And breathed for the first time,
And with a cry of protest, a bit of the air of the world,
 - We have been slowly dying little by little
Until we finally die and cease to exist.
And we always ask ourselves: is it really possible
That this is our life? Is it true that this is really it?
And occasionally we also ask ourselves secretly:
If our ancestral parents had not sinned
And had not been expelled from Eden,
Would they and we be living peacefully in the meadows?

For now, between birth and death
Between this and that
 - We live all the time in fleeting movements,
But almost never really restfully;
Because all our lives we try to achieve
Complete happiness, or at least
To find the security of our peace of mind;
And we always feel that we will not manage
To reach our life's goal by the end of the way;
In this path which – between us –

Also leads nowhere and to nothing;
Because our aim will already be, right after we die,
Nothing and naught.

And Man Discovered Awareness

No. God did not have to worry that the man and his wife,
Who had already learned to tell good from bad, would pick
Fruit from the tree of life in the Garden of Eden,
for after they ate of the fruit
– they were sentenced to be expelled, and they learned that
They were also sentenced to be mortal
in the world outside Eden.
(For up till then they were really ignorant, lacked awareness,
and guarded Eden without understanding, and acted like
robots carrying out God's commands).
But after eating from the forbidden fruit – they gained
awareness and discovered sex:
"the eyes of them both were opened,
and they knew that they were naked",
and they wore clothes, got to learn the difficulties of life,
and then they did not need the fruit from
the tree of life at all, as they learnt how to have children,
who would continue life, after they would
Return to dust upon their death.

Life of Methuselah

Indeed, the story of Methuselah is old,
But still today, it stands the test of time,
For what Methuselah, the oldest of men,
saw In his life, lasting 969 years.

So much was written and told
and will be spoken about for many days:
He was the great-grandchild of the great-grandchild of Seth,
Who was Adam and Eve's son;
He separated from his father, Enoch, when God took him,
And so he became an orphan, when he was already 300 years old;
He was happy when his son Lamech was born,
when he was 187 years,
And on his 369th year, he celebrated the
birth of his grandson, Noah,
But he cried, at the age of 964,
over the death of Lamech, his eldest son.
(Five years before Methuselah passed away and was buried),
But he ceased being sad when God loved his grandson,
And it was decided that Noah
was the only righteous man in his generation.

And since he lived another 600 years after the birth of his
grandson,
he was still strong physically and could see well.

He also witnessed the birth of his three great-grandchildren:
Shem, Ham, and Japheth, born to Noah, their father
When he was 500 years old.

And it is possible that Methuselah,
Son of the blessed dynasty of Seth
Passed away just before the flood, where
All the sinners - family members of the cursed
family of Cain - drowned and died,
And because of whom, God regretted creating man
And decided to wipe them all from the face of the earth.
For their intentions were evil, and they were very wicked.

Noah Asks

I was there,
But all that has happened
Has passed, no longer mentioned.
I will be here too,
But all that is due
To happen, I wish I knew.
Though I return to my land,
But still I wish to understand:

What will I still learn
After the apple
Was eaten, with the worm?

What can we still hope for
After the water gathered
And the shy, naked lands were discovered?

And what more can we do
After Cain's act of murder
And after the Lord set upon him the mark,
But build an altar,
Have some hearty alcohol,
Get drunk, and wait for what's coming.

Could It Be?

(Written in the middle of a rain and snow storm)

Could it be that this is the door to the abyss,
Which leads to hell
And not the gate to heaven?
And this rain, which has arrived early
To the branches of the almond trees;
And this rain, which has lasted two days already,
Will it be like last year's rain,
Or will it be another great flood,
Which, in spite of the creator's promise
Will turn all the lands
Into a seafloor?

And then summer, if it actually arrives,
Will it be like all summers
Or an end to all season?

Lot's Wife

You turned into a pillar of salt,
A statue with no defined location.
And that is quite a strange notion
As every statue placed in the square
Carries the name of a known hero there.
While you had neither name nor title
And you were not a heroine at all,
But a wife and a mother who was quite beastly
And gave up (maybe too easily) on her two daughters,
who were about to be gang-raped,
Which would lead, no doubt, to an awful end
By the crowd, the crowd of evil people,
Who then besieged your home in Sodom.

And you were also a woman who defied God's command
To flee without stopping, or turning around,
A woman sinning out of curiosity, like Pandora.
But, on the other hand, you may
Have missed your home, which you left straight away.
Or maybe you also had a sense of vengeance
For all they had done to you, those residents
Those evil, wicked people of Sodom.

And also, it is not completely clear to us
What kind of salt your statue is made of, thus:
Is it salt made of sodium chloride,
Or plaster made of calcium and sulphur?

Questions for Lot's Wife

Why did Lot's wife, who may have been sensitive,
Why did she look back and defy God's command?
Did she not think that God would punish her, as He
Is all-knowing, sees all that happens in the sea and land?

Or did she agree, earlier, to her husband's suggestion
To sacrifice her daughters to rape and death by Sodom's men?
Did she not know that to get to the top of the mountain
One must go only along the path leading ahead?

What did you see
Back there, Madam, please tell me.
You saw neither your home,
Nor the plain of Jordan,
But the fire and steam
From the evaporating river,
During the terrible overthrow
Of Sodom and Gomorrah.

A Thing and Its Opposite

After the horror of Sodom and Gomorrah:

"And the firstborn said unto the younger:
Our father is old, and there is not a man in the earth
to come in unto us after the manner of all the earth: Come, let
us make our father drink wine, and we will lie with him, that we
may preserve seed of our father."

(GENESIS 19: 31-32)

Good and evil, joy and terror
Firmness and weakness, positron and electron;
Matter and antimatter, finity and infinity;
Death and eternity, Lies and truth, Esau and Jacob.

""Escape for thy life, look not behind thee"
–The two angels in Sodom urged Lot,
Who suggested to the crowd that besieged his home
To rape his two daughters
In order to keep his two guests safe within their quarters;
Little did he know that some time ahead
His daughters **would rape him** night after night in his bed,
After giving him more and more wine
Till he fell asleep drunk;
And all this was to save and rescue humanity
From destruction.

Hagar (A Ballad)

"And Abraham rose up early in the morning and took bread and a bottle of water and gave it unto Hagar, putting it on her shoulder, and the child and sent her away; and she departed and wandered in the wilderness of Beer-Sheba."

(GENESIS, CHAPTER 21, VERSE 14)

He rose up early in the morning
And took bread
And a goatskin-bottle of water
And gave it unto Hagar,
Putting it on her shoulder.
As he sent her away
He dared not look her in the eye;
When he placed the child in her arms,
His face was pale with shame
As he thus sent them from their home.

She went on her way in the morning,
She went with the boy who was crying,
She went out there in the sun,
She went south to the wilderness
Wandering in the desert of Beer-Sheba,
The dry uncultivated waste land.
And when they finished the bread
And the water from the goatskin,

Then under one of the shrubs
She cast her own child.

She went and sat down over against him
A good way off, as it were a bow shot away,
With no strength left,
She sat there and wept,

For she said, let
Me not see my child's death.
And there was only the blazing sun,
With a quiet crying of the child,
So that only God could hear
And salvage a dying lad.

Woman of Valour

"Who can find a woman of valour?"

(PROVERBS 31:10)

Who can find a woman of valour?
A woman of valour, who will find her?
 – We men will look for her in vain
And we will not find her
Even if we look again and again.

Who can find a woman of valour?
A woman of valour, who will find her?
 -Since Abraham, we men will never find her,
Because the ram that will be offered instead
 – Will never come.

Moses the Prophet at an Eye Clinic

"And the Lord spake unto Moses face to face."

(EXODUS 33:11)

Perhaps this is what the doctor said to Moses, the Prophet,
At The eye clinic in the field hospital,
Set up near the oasis, Kadesh Barnea:
"After seeing God face-to-face at the top of Mount Sinai,
It is no wonder that you say you have pain in your eyes.
Anyway, if I were to summarize
We found that in both your eyes
The cornea is clear, the pupils are round
And responsive, there's a light irritation in the conjunctiva,
The lens is clear, but has some erosion of slight murkiness.

Apart from these light ailments
Your eyes are quite good
And you'll be able to see the Promised Land
When you climb up Mount Nebo
To look at it, but to it you shan't go.

Phalti, Son of Laish

About the man who cried for the love of a woman.

(2 SAMUEL, 3:15)

Phalti, the son of Laish,
Did well, and had goats that were brownish.
One day, men took his gorgeous
Wife, the princess,
And his pride was totally crushed.

He cried and went after her,
But she didn't look behind her,
So they ordered him thus:
Go home, no more fuss,
And he did, so defeated and ashamed.

This poem's about Phalti, y' understand
A landlord, a respectable man.
Till he married a femme fatale:
It was princess Michal,
And he became a most miserable man.

Go learn from the man's bitter end
Humiliated to the ground, to the grave:
Never wed
A princess, but dread
The idea, and flee far, far away.

Four Verses on a Biblical Hero

"And... was Shamgar, the son of Anat... which slew the Phillistines
six hundred men with an ox goad and also delivered Israel"
(JUDGES 3:31)

There once was a man who was mighty,
Before going to sleep in his nighty
- He killed Philistines
Six-hundred by means
Which still no one knows how exactly.

What is the name of this wild hero
Who fought, certain odds close to zero,
With ox-goad for cows
Alone was aroused
And still no one knows who's this hero.

In the Book of Judges appears he,
In only one verse written clearly,
And we still know naught
Today more about
This hero who hit so distinctly.

His name was Shamgar, the son of Anat, he
Dispersed Philistines all about thee
With ox-goad for tool
He hit them quite cruel
– It's written there ever so clearly.

She Shall Not Come Rejoicing, the Bearer of His Sheaves

And the army unit "took her...from Phaltiel the son of Laish. And her husband went with her along weeping behind her."

(2 SAMUEL 3:15-16).

"He that goeth forth and weepeth, bearing precious seed, shall doubtless come again with rejoicing, bringing his sheaves with him."

(PSALMS 126:6)

Under the roof of the mansion Galim,
Lived master Phaltiel, son of Laish
And Princess Michal, his wife,
Who never let him touch her,
For she still loved David, her first husband,
Whom she smuggled out on the eve of their wedding,
And so saved him from the hands of the murderers,
Sent by her father, Saul
Who wanted to kill him.

And when his wife was taken from him forcefully
Something he would not have imagined
Even in his worst nightmare,
– Her husband Phaltiel followed her,
A long way and long cry
Bearing precious seed –
Who went forth and wept

After Princess Michal
Who never looked back at him.

He knew that
She would not return to him,
He also knew that she would never bear his sons,
And he knew that she is not and will not
Come rejoicing, bringing his sheaves with her.

Jephthah's Daughter

"And she went... and bewailed her virginity upon the mountains..."
(BOOK OF JUDGES 11:38)

In the autumn, that autumn, the girl went to the mountains
To cry with her companions, not just over her virginity
But also because of her forthcoming death
When she would be sacrificed by her own father,
To be the first human sacrifice in Israel.
In the autumn, in the autumn before that
Then too she went to the mountains,
But then she was a girl of laughter:
She made a bouquet for the festival of youth
Of leaves from trees and flowers from bushes
Which shamelessly fell on her head
Due to her laughter and blossoming youth.
But that autumn
All the leaves on the trees wilted
And fell then with endless amazement,
As no one would save them
From the echo of her weeping, from that echo
That rose from the mountains
As it wandered but also protested
Her fate that autumn,
Her twilight hour.

Why was Uzzah, Son of Abinadab, Killed?

"And the anger of the Lord was kindled against Uzzah; and God smote him there."

(2 SAMUEL 6:7)

Why was Uzzah, son of Abinadab, from Gibeha, beaten and killed?
He and his brother carried the Ark of the Lord from their home In a new wagon, pulled along by cattle
To the city of David, in Jerusalem; and David and all the people
Gathered around the ark, playing drums and harps, and dancing
Till they reached the granary. It is true that
On the way the ark dropped, due to a fault of the cattle;
But he, Uzzah, son of Abinadab, was the only one who dared to hold the Ark of the Lord and to put it back in the wagon.

And why was God angry? (*"and God smote him... and there he died"*).
What mistake did Uzzah make?
Was it because he was not a priest, but a member of the tribe of Levi? Should someone else have done it instead?
Even David was angry that God *"had made a breach upon Uzzah"*
And moreover, *"he called the name of the place **Perez-uzzah** to this day"*.

Rizpah, Daugter of Aiah (A Ballad)

(The fate of Rizpah, daughter of Aiah, was tragic. Rizpah was the concubine of King Saul, and after he died on Mount Gilboa, Abner, Son of Ner, took her (probably against her will), to be his mistress. Rizpah had two sons with Saul, and they were sentenced to be hanged, as demanded by the Gibeonites, to avenge Saul's family for killing their priests by the king's army, as commanded by him. Rizpah covered the bodies of her two sons hanging from the wall, and guarded them, day and night, throughout the summer, so that their bodies would not be eaten by predators. Till finally rain started falling, and King David agreed to bury the dead sons.)

(2 SAMUEL, 3:7), (2 SAMUEL, 21: 8-11)

And the sun stood still upon Gibeon;
When the king's sons were killed there,
Sons of the concubine, Rizpah, daughter of Aiah.
They were hanged on the tops of Mount Saul
The young men, Armoni and Mephibosheth
So that their corpses would be seen by all -
So that they should see them and beware.

In Gibeon the sun was already setting
About to create the evening
So one man asked the other:
"Shall the sword devour forever?"
Will there always be a blood-feud here?

And his friend replied thus:
"Soon it will be dark.
The moon has a halo around it.
Fate is maddening Rizpah
And death devoured her sons."
So the first man added and said:
"In the days of King Ishbosheth,
(The only son of Saul who survived
And was crowned after the fight on Mount Gilboa),
The commander-in-chief of his army abused her
While she was mourning Saul.
He took Rizpah by force.
When Ishbosheth then went to Abner
To avenge the mistress's honour,
He was murdered during nap time.
Showers fell from the skies,
And the windows of heaven were opened
Just as they did then,
At the start of the great flood."

So his friend then replied,
As they walked through the meadow:
"Happy is the passer-by, wanderer
Who is far from greatness and power,
But why should the downtrodden suffer
Like the concubine Rizpah, daughter of Aiah,
Who had such a cruel end.

Her fate did not do her justice.
She gained neither honour nor happiness."

And the mistress Rizpah, daughter of Aiah,
Sat there, with her two sons,
Who were dead, hanging from wooden boards.
She guarded them day and night,
And covered them with sacks,
So that birds of prey should not eat their flesh,
So that field animals should not harm them.

She sat there facing them, without a barrier
With barely any bread and water.
She protected their bodies from harm,
She guarded them throughout the summer,
Till rain started falling,
Till David took pity on her,
And let her sons be buried.

Michal, Saul's Daughter

Michal ,Saul's daughter, who loved David so much
And announced it, so the world would know;
Michal, for whom David paid two hundred foreskins
Was his wife for only half of the night of their wedding,
As she smuggled him out of the window, away from killers.
Married Michal, whose father married her again,
To a stranger, to Phalti, to avenge her actions.
She never forsook David, her love;
And though she was wed to two,
She never had a son or daughter of her own.

Love-sick Princess Michal, you see
Grew up and was a haughty lady.
When later, she looked out of the window
And despised David with all her heart seeing him dance
around the Torah ark
(And even went out and reprimanded him with her remarks),
And perhaps that is why she
Never fulfilled her femininity,
For she had no child of her own
And died all alone.

Abishag

(1 Kings 1:3)

And if King David
Was to be old –
Give him a woman who is a beauty to behold.
Find him Abishag the Shunammite,
Who will keep him warm and offer him tenderness
At the end of his days.

And since King David was sentenced
To leave this world
And in a while to lie with his ancestors,
Pay him for his life's work,
And find him the fairest
On his way to dust.

Please Sit Down

Please sit down in your house,
And stay there when you sleep and when you rouse;
And when you sit in your lounge,
And when you lie down, sleepless, in your bed,
And when you go to other rooms instead,
Where you will examine your life,
You will not always remember how and what you did
When you reflect on the way you lived.

Dear King David:
Your back is already bent, your body – cold,
You are now very old.
Therefore, enjoy your last day and night
With Abishag the Shunammite
Till your day from God arrives.

Athaliah

"And... [Athaliah] arose and destroyed all the royal seed."

(2 KINGS 11:1).

Leave, leave already, Athaliah, you bloody woman,
evil- minded queen.
Leave to the house of God, to your death, which you so deserve,
wicked person and murderess!
For we can still hear the sound of the blood of your
grandchildren, right in the depths of our brains.
They cry to us from the ground,
Over which you, heinous woman, walk around.
Your death will now arrive after you committed the sin of pride,
And greed for rule and power.

And your name will be damned forever, just as the name of
your mother, Jezebel, is damned.
For you have spilled much blood in the land,
For you swayed the heart of your husband, Jehoram, to do
evil, and to worship Baal and Astarte;
After his death, and the death of your son, Ahaziah, kings of
Judah – you chose to rule the land alone.
You murdered your grandchildren just so you could rule, and
be such an evil tyrant
(Unlike Greek Medea, who murdered her two sons to avenge
her adulterous husband, Jason).

Indeed, the land was then filled with abomination and killings,
that the land hadn't seen in many years:
Starting with Elijah the prophet, who, in the Kishon River,
slew four hundred and fifty of the prophets of Baal.
Then, your mother, Jezebel, stole the vineyard of Naboth
"the Jezreelite," and brought about his death, all through lies,
To Jehu, who defied King Ahab, and ordered the palace
eunuchs to kill Jezebel by throwing her out of the window, and
destroyed all the house of Ahab, and displayed their chopped
heads in the square, as if they were flags.

But you were most evil of all, for you had no pity for your
own offspring, and as such you murdered your grandchildren!
If it weren't for the infant Jehoash, the grandchild hidden in
the house of God, who was saved from your turning blade,
Then all seed of the kingdom of the house of David would
have been lost, after it had lasted for generations.
And when he turned seven, he was crowned in the temple.
And furthermore, Jehoiada the priest and men of the guard
plotted against you;
And now, when you come to the temple, they will take you
out, and, in front of the horses of the guard, will kill you with
a sword.

Verses on the Book of Esther

Over a hundred and twenty seven states
Ahasuerus ruled and dictated,
But over his wife, Vashti,
In the chambers of his harem,
He could not rule,
Which he thought would come naturally.

In the kingdom of Persia, Ethiopia and India,
When awaiting the selection of a beauty queen,
Out of brown-skinned, light-skinned and dark-skinned girls,
Only Esther had grace unseen.

So the king then said: "I love her,
She's the fairest of all, she's a treasure
Put a crown on her head
She'll be queen now instead
And my new wife will give me much pleasure.

So he held a feast in a hall
To present Esther to all
But only she knew
That her father was a Jew
– She didn't tell him at all.
Then came the conspirators
Bigthan and Teresh

Who may have been sent by Zeresh
That is Haman's wife
Who all her life
Wished they'd start again afresh

Mordecai sat alone at the gate
An 'intelligence' guy, not illiterate
So, as knowledge is power
He handed them over
Just doing his job, though so quiet.

So Mordecai, from the Tribe of Benjamin
Said to Esther: "Now, listen, cousin
Your king will clearly
Be murdered, you'll see
If about them you don't complain!"

Thus, Esther then went to the King
And told him about everything;
The sentence for the Jews she cancelled,
Shushan giggled and chuckled,
And day and night they celebrated.

That's the end of Haman, son of Hammedatha,
Evil man, and father of Vaizatha;
All in Shushan did repeat
The word in the street
That they would all then be hanged by their feet.

He is the Ruler

He who made
The eels that always
Slip my hands...

He who fixed
In my somber sky
Mocking moon to accuse...

He who set
Rules and measures
For the righteous...

He has now lit
Lasting lights
In my upturned eyes,

For He has ruled
That my wife will weave
Out in the open
All my white shrouds.

A Still Small voice

"... The Lord passed by...(in) a still small voice."

(I KINGS 19, 11-12)

A great and strong wind came
And rent the mountains,
And after the wind came an earthquake
And broke in to pieces the rocks,
Then came a fire that burnt it all.

But the Lord was not in the wind,
Neither was He in the earthquake
Nor in the fire,
Because the Lord passed by
In a still small voice.

Poems on Cain and Abel

Burial of the Truth

"And Cain was very wroth, and his countenance fell..."

(Genesis, 4:2)

...And already he plans
The time
When he would carry a spade
To bury
The body of truth
In the ground too.

But the earth would not cover it,
As the truth would out,
Whether by a sign
From above,
Or by a loud and bitter cry,
Bursting straight from the ground.

If I Am My Brother`s Keeper

"Am I my brother's keeper ?"

(GENESIS 4:9)

If Abel is my brother,
Then his brother I am as well,
Since brothers we are.

And if I am my own brother's keeper,
 - Selfish I am not,
As I do not keep me
From myself...

Alas, I am REALLY not...
My own brother.

Cain's Serial Numbers

You were the first to be born
And the first to bring an offering,
Then you were the first to be angry
And you became the first murderer
And the first one to deny it.

But you were warned second,
After your father;
And you were questioned third,
After your father and mother;
And you were cursed fourth,
After your father, your mother
And the snake.

The Criminal Dynasty of Cain

"Fortunate is the man who has never tasted God's vengeance!"
Wrote Sophocles in the play *Antigone,*
And even our God repented
The creation of man:
For *"the wickedness of man was great in the earth, and that every imagination of the thoughts of his heart was only evil continually";*
– These are God's words.
Thus he drowned all humans in the flood
(Except the family of Noah who *"found grace in the eyes of the Lord"*).

That was also the bitter end of Cain's dynasty
Whose offspring were all sinners and master criminals,
Such as Lamech, son of Methusael, the killer poet,
Who informed Adah and Zillah, his two wives
That in his grief he had murdered two;
And this he told in rhyming verse
Lamech – Cain's great-grandchild's grandchild.

And You Shall Not Rule It

And the Lord said unto Cain:
"Sin lieth at the door.
*Unto thee shall be his desire, **and thou shalt rule over him.**"*

But thou, young man, shan't rule it
because you are too young.

Every morning, the sin too wakes up and lies at the door,
But you, grown man, shall not once rule over it.

The sin has been lying in the strong sun for a long time,
But you, old man, shall not see it nor rule over it.

Night falls, and the death penalty is already hovering over the
sin, but you, elderly man, still do not notice it.

For from the beginning until your final day
The sin will always lie at the door of your life,
And you, who went wandering around the world,
  - **Shall never truly rule over it.**

Blues for Cain

Ok Cain,
Accept the fact,
That no one loved you
In the small world of ancient times.
It is very doubtful, whether your mother Eve loved you
True mother's love.
It is very doubtful, whether Adam, your father,
Really loved you.
It is crystal clear that Abel, your brother
Really did not love you.
Since you were a tiller of the soil,
How could you be loved and spoiled?
- As you worked and lived close to your parents
And they saw you daily and saw your caprices.
That is why they preferred Abel, your brother,
The shepherd who, with his goats and sheep would roam
And only occasionally come back home.
This naturally made his parents' longing grow
And gave the flames of love a brighter glow.

Even God did not find you pleasing,
See here: He would not accept your offering.
Furthermore – he often preached to you
But you would not listen to him or take his advice.

And how, if at all, could you be loved, worker of the land
Which was cursed by God, because of what you and your
father, had done?
As it was written: *"Thorns also and thistles shall it bring forth to
thee"*; it is with sadness that you shall eat bread, by the sweat
of your brow, until you return to the ground,
Since you were taken from it, for you are dust.

What Satan could have said to Cain?

In memory of Isaac Rabin, the Israeli prime minister,
Killed by a fanatic Jew on 5 November 1995.

"When you killed Abel you helped me very much,
Since you killed a quarter of humanity
And made my work very easy,
As I am only a beginner-Satan.

But why did you not know that his blood,
Which still cries from the ground,
Contains iron enough to make six nails?
And how could you not know that the phosphor of his body
Could turn into matches filling ten boxes?
And didn't you know that the salt spread in his flesh
Could fill a medium plate?
To say nothing of the possibility of exploiting his hide and hair,
Not to mention the most precious hormones.

But one thing you did not know that makes me really angry:
That from his bones it was possible to make talismans,
Which are very important gadgets
In my public-relations campaign!"

If I Were Not a Tiller of the Land

If I were not a tiller of the land,
Maybe my offering would be accepted there too;
If I had not then killed Abel, my only brother
 - I would not be a murderer,
Nor a liar nor a vagabond;
And I would not be, after both my parents,
The third sinner,
And I would not be remembered
As the one who spilled Abel's blood,
And my offspring would also
Not have died in the terrible flood.

If I were not Cain,
A farmer and land owner
 - I would also not then
Be a real estate man and a contractor
Who would build his son a city named after him.
But, to my dismay, I was that real Cain
And I killed Abel my only brother, out of jealously;
And for that I was the first murderer in the history of man.
But in spite of everything,
I fulfilled what Solomon ordered in Proverbs
For every father: *"train up a child in the way he should go"*
As I built the city Enoch – in his name.

Abel

You were the second man to be born
In the world outside the Garden of Eden,
And as fate had it, you were destined to be a shepherd
In a green land, with pasture aplenty.
You were a naïve and honest man
With pure eyes that did not see any evil,
As you had a good heart from your youth.

As a naïve man, you learnt from your elder brother
How to give offerings of gratitude to the world's creator,
But He did not accept Cain's offer,
And Cain then filled with jealousy and anger
As God would rather
Have the offering of the younger brother.

What, then, did you reply to jealous Cain
When he came to you then
And into a temper flew,
Shouting insult and abuse,
Before he rose up and killed you?

What a pity, Abel
That we could not have heard
Your last words.

Maybe you answered him, incidentally,
That it would be a pity if hatred and jealousy,
Would always live together
With love and faith, and would be forever
Inside people's souls.

Poems on Samson

Samson, Son of Manoah

A man named Samson
Was born to be a Nazirite to God Almighty.

A man named Samson
Aimed to free Israel from the Philistines.

A man called Samson
Did not abstain from the Philistine women.

A man called Samson
Was a very strong hero thanks to his hair, so long.

The one and only man
Whose name was Samson, son of Manoah*,
Though he was a fearsome fellow
He could not find peace in his life, ah!
–Till he killed many Philistines
(For he knew only the language of power).
And the people he killed
When his death was near
Were even more than those he'd killed
In all the previous years.

* Note: The name Ma-no-ah means also in Hebrew -
a peaceful rest (a common noun).

Samson's Love

*"And he came up, and told his father and his mother, and said, I
have seen a woman in Timnath of the daughters of the Philistines:
now therefore get her for me to wife. Then his father and his mother
said unto him, [is there] never a woman among the daughters of
thy brethren, or among all my people, that thou goest to take a
wife of the uncircumcised Philistines?"*

(JUDGES 14:2-3)

Even if I were a monk –
I would visit her every night
And every night – I would taste her honey.

Even if I were a prisoner –
I would ask for her every night
And every night – in a deep sweet dream.

Even if I were a nomad–
I would chase her every night
And every night - I would run amok.
If only to spread my arms,
Like the wings of eagles and kites,
Then my legs would carry me, light as deer,
Just to her, the foreign maiden.

Because maybe only with her would I find some happiness
And some comfort from the troubles of our oppressed people,
And maybe only with her would I also be fit
To kill the conquering Philistines,
If only for the next generation.

Of Hair and all the Rest

Sometimes it was good, sometimes it was bad,
But his hair was always wet.
Sometimes he was here, sometimes there,
But he always shampooed his hair.

Sometimes he rested, sometimes he moved,
But his hair was always subdued.

He always knew it, in advance,
That his hair would become less dense.

He just wanted to bring the message home
That his hair would be eternally combed.

This is a poem on Samson's hair at best
With only a hint about the rest.

This poem has just commenced
And here it absolutely ends.

I Am an Anti-Hero

I admit and confess:
I could not, like Samson the hero
Kill thirty people in Ashkelon <u>two days ago</u>
In order to remove their clothes from them
And give them to those who solve the riddle as a reward;
And also like him when I went <u>yesterday</u> to a harlot in Gaza
And I could not do it - she comforted me and said:
"Don't make a big deal of it, it's not so bad".
Is it any wonder that even <u>today</u>
I cannot regrow hair on my bald head
Or, like him, topple the hall pillars.

But what a pity that <u>now</u> I really
Am not, like him, a monk who does not abstain
From relations with foreign women.

Meditative Poems

The Coordinates of Place and Time

(Written in Jerusalem, Israel, on November 22nd, 1999)

Here comes so close to us
The end of the second millennium,
With the end of the twentieth century;
And we were already born,
Somewhere and sometime,
In this turbulent century -
And we will be soon people of ancient time...

And we live here, north of the equator,
On the thirty-two degrees latitude
And on the thirty-five degrees longitude
East of Greenwich and the Mediterranean sea,
In the big continent named Asia,
That is located on our huge planet Earth,
Which is the third planet of our solar system,
In the very long galaxy of the Milky Way,
Which is only one of millions of galaxies
Existing in the endless cosmos,
And are constantly running away,
One from the other with accelerating speed...

So we already have no choice
But, perhaps, be consoled by the fact
That even the just-born baby will be like us:
A member of this passing old century.

This Is the Time and This Is the Place

Man, man, where art thou?
- I exist, here in the area.
I am ready and waiting and am here on time.
Man, man, is all this certain?
- Look: Here I am in this place and at this time:
On the first day of the month of Ramadan, in the year 1422
Of the Hijra immigration of the Prophet Muhammad;
On the seventh of November, in the year 2002
After the birth of Christ, Son of God, and the Messiah;
At the beginning of the month of Kislev, the year 5763 to the
creation of the world, as in the Old Testament;
In the city of Tel Aviv, 32 and a half degrees latitude north
of the equator, meeting with 35 degrees longitude, east of
Greenwich, England.
And I am here, in this place and at this time, and I am ready
and waiting – **For your command.**

Time Definitions

"To everything there is a season, and a time to every purpose under the heaven."

(ECCLESIASTES 3:1)

a.

Time measures the duration of all events
And the periods between them;
Time measures the rate of the changes
Which always take place;
Time flows in one direction only
So it really is used, And it always is used
To distinguish between what there was and what there is,
And what is about to take place.

b.

Time is also measured with the hands of the clock
Which shows seconds, minutes, and hours.
And it always has a present, which is a quick intermediate
period, a very tiny particle, between the time that has passed
and the time in the future;
And it is like a bird passing overhead, its shadow passing with it.
Time also moves to the rhythm of an 'internal clock' in animals:
(The rhythm of time of a year in a dog's life equals seven
human years of life).
Time also has a mental expression: it is fastest in dangerous
situations, dreadful or traumatic.
And remarkably slow in conditions of inactivity and idleness.

Place, Time and Light (PTL)

A place is something defined
Between both axes on the map.
A place marks a specific area,
Or some unknown, to our forefathers.
A place is something in the wide open space,
Which exists, like the plain of Jordan or Mountain Nebo.
In Hebrew, God is also referred to as 'the place'
To whom so many people pray.

Time marks the duration of things
And measures changes in events;
And time only moves forward,
And never goes backwards.

Light, too, moves swiftly ahead,
As light travels in waves;
And light, sometimes, comes from afar
From a distant, long gone, star.

But if we would fly ahead at the speed of light
Both we and time would go backwards;
We would return to our place of birth,
When we began our existence.

Takings

What did the mother toad
Take from the little tadpole that lived in the water,
Which hatched out of a soft egg
In a large string, laid in the water?

She did not take with her
His gills or his tail
When she left for dry land.
But she took his vitality with her
To be a mature and different amphibian.

What did the butterfly
Which hatched from the chrysalis,
Which was once a caterpillar,
Which hatched from
A butterfly's egg,
- What did it take?

It took antenna
And it took eyes,
As well as scales and wings
And most important: it took
Another shape.

What did Eve, the woman,
Take from the first man, Adam,
Who was made from the soil
In the likeness, and after the image
Of his creator?

She took one of his ribs
And was created to be
An help meet for him.
Then she took his naiveté
To be a mother to all living from his seed,
And to know, more than she then could
What is bad and what is good.

Things as They Are

a.

If a woman is about to give birth to a girl
 - The girl will then be
Her fetus inside a woman
Who became pregnant by her man,
Who is just a man.

c.

A man is a male,
Created in a woman's womb,
Who, on his way to becoming a father,
Also tries in vain
To return to his mother's womb
Through the piping system of another woman.

Time of Life

When a baby is born –
Immediately the arrow of his life is shot
From the bow of a mother's womb
To something unknown
Called life, which naturally grows
And reacts to changes and different events,
Like sound and light, the touch of cold and heat;
Life which takes materials from its environment
To absorb them into its body;
Life which multiplies and has offspring,
Who continue to sustain their species;
Life which ends sometimes, for that is its nature.

But throughout life
Time is a relative thing:
Now or later, fast or slow;
A long, or short period.
Yesterday is in the past,
Tomorrow is in the future,
Now is in the present,
Such a mini-minute length of time;
Less than a pulse beat,
Or the batting of an eyelid.
For it is infinitesimal
And continuously approaches zero as a limit.

Rise and Call

(To Arieh Shalev, my dear brother)

"What meanest thou, o sleeper? Arise, call upon thy God"
(JONAH I, 6)

Here and now you are a man,
Now and here a man you are,
Because there is no one who is placeless
Neither there is one who is timeless.

Here is the place and now is your time,
Now is the time and here is your place,
Then why do you slumber, man?
- Arise and call!

Everyone Has a Life of a River

Everyone has a life of a river
To which its tributaries are his parents,
That have gathered him together
From a wide area,
In which they have streamed,
Gently and sometimes stormy,
Until they have given him his life,
A life full of joy as of fresh waters.

And in his days of youth
He rows himself a channel,
He builds himself two banks
And still he has time to have fun
And sometimes even to be naughty.

But when he is mature enough
Striving to broaden its flow
- He sweeps away his steep banks,
He does not rake more pebbles
Nor deepens his channel.

And in his old age
His flow is very slow,
He is already very lonely and sleepy,
With his face covered he stretches his arms in a delta
And he is simply finished by merging
into the wide deep sea.

What Does the Embryo Dream about?

What does a human embryo dream about,
Sleeping most of the time in his mother's womb?
Does he dream there,
About the adventures and transformations
That he has been through
Throughout his development?
– From a micro-organism to a small fish,
To a tadpole and then to an amphibian,
To a chick, to a calf – till he resembles a human.

What does the human embryo dream about,
As he floats in the warm amniotic fluid
And receives nutrients and oxygen from the bloodstream?
Does he kick when he dreams,
Because of nightmares?
Does he also laugh in his dreams
Already there, in his mother's womb,
At the irony of fate?

To Agree or Disagree
(A questionnaire)

Do you strongly disagree
To swim in the open sea?

Do you simply disagree
To fall off the backs of horses?

Do you neither agree nor disagree
To join the armed forces?

Do you slightly agree
To speak the truth and see
That you remain honest to a degree
As a man can be?

Do you simply agree
That you can now fall in love
And sing along with the dove
Under the somber skies above?

Do you strongly agree
With what you inside really feel
That faith in God will really heal?

Do you neither agree nor disagree
That happiness could be reached by decree?

The Rest of Our Lives

"Were the world and man indeed created in six days,
While, later, the first man lived nine hundred and thirty years
And the world – i.e. earth – has existed for at least 4.6 billion years"?

(DAVID STILLMAN)

If indeed two days ago it was the sixth day
– The day we were created,
And if yesterday, the **Sabbath,**
The day our creator
Rested from all His work,
Was also the time of our maturity
And the day we become knowledgeable;
Then today, **Sunday,**
From sunrise to sunset
Is the first day
Of the rest of our lives.

And **tomorrow**
Will be a day too late for us,
For it will be the time of our old age;
Not just another 'in the meantime' day,
Not just an 'in-between' day,
But the day before we die
On the following day.

The Nature of Man

According to observations and scientific experiments,
It seems the nature of man
Hasn't changed over the years,
And his soul has always been governed
By certain rules.
Thus, man fears the dark.
His soul full of hallucinations, nonsense, miracles,
For he is not aware
That darkness is like a fossilized fire,
Imprisoned in the rock In bones, long extinct
In natural or man-made disasters.
The nature of man
Was determined from the days of Adam
And his three sons: Cain, Abel and Seth.

The Women Who Await Their Men's Return

Michal loved David her first husband, and awaited his return.
Even when she was in "Galim", the estate of Palti,
Her second husband, whom she married under the orders of
Saul, her father, who punished her.
Solveig also waited for her love, Peer Gynt, for a long time,
As did Penelope, queen of Ithaca, who waited
Twenty years for the return of her husband, Odysseus.

Who are these, and other women, waiting for,
And why do they yearn for them and wait for many years
For their beloved men to return?
– As it is not certain at all
Whether they deserve this yearning.
For men are not built for long-term loneliness,
And cannot contain the sperm they produce all the time,
Thus they will not hold it in their bodies,
Over the years when they are very far from home,
And will betray their wives, who yearn so for their return.

Who Is the Real 'I'?

("If I am not for myself who is for me? And being for my own self, what am I?" -Rabbi Hillel).

First of all, the baby knows his parents, and calls them, wrongly.
Then he will name close objects, like a bottle and a dummy;
And then he will notice the light, the sun, the sky, the clouds,
the birds and the tree, and will fear the dark night,
But then he will also discover the stars.

And only after he loudly says "no" and "mine",
He will acknowledge his own existence and also say "I",
And then, all his young and mature years,
He will wonder who that "I" of his is:
Is it just his physical body?
Or is it his consciousness too?
Does that also express its meaning?
Is it his memory, his wishes and hopes?
Are they his being, his past and his future?
Is he the one who builds his personality himself?
Does he need to strengthen the "I", as he fears his end?

Is there someone in the world
who will tell him who his real "I" is?

What Was to be Proven

"And Michal...loved David"

(I SAMUEL, 18:20)

What was to be proven,
What was to be shown,
 Will it be proven as much as possible
And shown as much as is feasible.

Overlooking the price
("Whatever the cost"),
Ignoring what will be tomorrow
("Whatever happens – happens").

For what truly matters,
Is that you do love each other,
And only that shows
That you really do exist.

Who, What and Where

Who were we, I wonder,
and what are we, I ask?
and who on earth were we
and what on earth are we
and for what are we
and where are we going from here?
- I keep wondering
And I am still questioning.

Are we all God's children
Always sinning
Yet asking for forgiveness?
Do we all face
That final place,
 Somewhere in outer space,
Which we call 'there',
Fearing it is far from fair?

Who, what and where?
- I keep asking here and there,
But get no answer,
As no one seems to care...

Mythical and legendary verses

Gilgamesh

You were the son of a goddess and the king of Uruk,
You were two thirds a god and a third a mighty man,
In so many cruel and heartless acts you partook,
Because of which, you never did gain eternal life,
despite your personal plan...

You set off to desolate places with your friend, Enkidu,
To Utnapishtim, survivor of the Great Flood,
To ask the wise man if he would
Offer advice as to how one could
Gain eternal life.
And though on the way you killed the Bull of Heaven
And also Humbaba, who in the cedar forest was a guardian,
And you sailed in a boat on the sea of death
Without touching its lethal waters;

And you tried, as advised by Utnapishtim,
Not to sleep at all for seven nights and days,
 - None of these things helped you:
The same snake who seduced Eve Our Mother,
Also stole the branch of the underwater plant
From you, which was supposed to grant

You eternal life,
- And because of that, when it later shed his skin
It did not die, but really lived again without you...

Oh, Gilgamesh,
Gilgamesh, King of Uruk,
Why did you get enmeshed
In such actions? As although you were mighty
And a king of valuable opinions,
- You did not know you would never be
Able to obtain eternal life.

Antigone (A Ballad)

As the night was wrapping Thebes,
With the silence already butchered by hidden crickets,
Facing the city wall rested the corpse -
The body of the dead Polynices,
Was silvered by the light of the moon.
The armed guards were watching it,
As the decree of the king
Was that it shall not be buried.

The night was swallowing Thebes.
After the moon had set
You came alone in the dark, Antigone.
You came to carry your dead brother,
To carry his corpse to the grave.
A sandstorm first raised hope your deed may be hidden
Alas, the heavens were determined
It should be revealed.

This moral obligation, Antigone,
You finally executed
With all the might of your conviction,
Against the strict order of your uncle, the king.
You were young, Antigone, very young,
Your life was with full songs of hope
You always chanted,

Until your resolution to bury your brother,
Until you opted for death.

You were young, Antigone, very young,
You were in love, Antigone , and beloved,
Betrothed to Haemon, the royal prince,
But you cast behind your happiness
By standing up against that order
Which was a sacrilege of your faith,
So the cave of fate opened its mouth
And there you were swallowed to death.

Oh Antigone, Antigone,
With such devotion, Antigone,
You fulfilled your obligation, Antigone.
Young and old mourn you, Antigone:
Oh Antigone, Antigone.

Socrates' Death

When they brought him the glass of poison
Socrates was still discussing the question
Of one's soul immortality.

And though he was already seventy years old
He was still barefooted, poor and clever,
As in his youth; and was still absorbed
With pondering his reasoning for arguments
About the soul of mankind.

And certainly as in his youth,
At this time too, people would call after him:
Socrates, Socrates,
Give us more knowledge,
Only a little more knowledge
– To at least know ourselves!

And thus, when the cold was rising from his legs
To reach his heart, he still persevered
To console man's soul
And make it good.

Honi the Encicler

Introduction:

Honi the Encircler lived in Israel in the first century BC. He was called the Encircler because in a drought year he would draw a circle, stand at its centre and declare: "Lord of Creation, I will not budge from here until you have mercy on your children" - whereupon it would begin to rain. Honi is said to have fallen asleep for 70 years and, upon awakening, found himself in a completely alien world.

You who in the days of the king Hyrkanos the second
Were known as the one adept at miracles,
What do you know today?
Now, after your long sleep, as you return
To the graves of your forefathers,
To lie down with your forebears,
What do you remember?
Whom do you know,
That from the days of the King
Still remembers your greatness?
Do you really think
That because of your prayers at the crossroads,
The prayers lifted from the center
And answered by rains in the days of drought,
- That you are in a world redeemed?
You, who are unknown today, unrecognized,
Having returned after seventy hoary years

To the bored sleep of the complacent -
To look for the new - listen carefully:
The world will remain round,
Even without yourself
No less than that old circle you once drew.
At night will still be heard
The snuffle of the sneezing goat
And dawn will rise like a tired bird
Trailing morning's pallor
For a painful clarity.
And at noon, to the sound of croaking frogs
In the ditch of muddy water,
There will be a slaughter
Of the sacrificial bird of paradise
(As though you had never lived -
As if there had been
No circle, no awakening,
No new yearning).
Now you are as good as dead,
Unloved, unknown,
Rushing around to find you,
Addled, confused,
With a heart that is everyone's target -
Bloated with words that your tongue does not utter.
As you pass through the market of good deeds
You notice what a modest turnover there is,
How cautious the buyers are.

Your figure is bowed down
Like a wall crawling with lizards,
Your blood is no longer laden
With a heavy load of iron,
You easily go down, on all fours,
As if desiring to be drained of you,
But do not worry:
The custodian of souls
Is about to come
Any moment, now.

A Return Visit to the Garden of Eden

Farewell all who live in the garden with no shame or sadness;
So long, animals residing on the ground, in bushes and grasses;
Farewell, birds on the oak trees, goodbye crocuses,
 - We protected you all from any evil there should be,
But we ourselves were not careful and ate the fruit of the tree.

Tomorrow morning we will be there, far away,
And we will call out loudly: "farewell, dream!"
Tomorrow we will probably not part, it seems
With the tree of life and its daily routine.

A Visit by the Well-Known Angel

(Was written at purim Festival, March 5th, 2015)

When the very well-known angel
Will come to take the soul of an unknown poet,
The poet will plead for his life:
"Give me five more minutes to breathe"
(Just like in the famous song:
"Give me five minutes more"...)

Then the notorious angel will ask:
"What did you do
On the fifth of March, 2015
Apart from writing this
Nonsensical poem?"
 - So you should have guessed
That I would stop the movement of your chest
And send you down –
To collapse in the black hole.

Another Reincarnation

He got up
From his old death,
Put on
A worn shoe on his foot,
Wore
A large hat on his head,
Dressed in his old uniform,
Forcefully opened
His locked door;

And (like all mortals do
Every morning) he let
A new spirit into his room
That this time too
(Just like in days of yore)
 - Did not bring with it
The sounds of rain.

Perhaps I Was Once A Stream

Perhaps I was once a stream of delights,
That flowed slowly, hesitantly,
Through ravines of loess hills,
Which started flowing thanks to some rain,
That fell in this country only now and again.

Or perhaps I was once also a strong stream,
Flowing among sections of mountains,
Which may have been formed
Before the covenant with Abraham Our Father.
Or perhaps I was also just a small, abandoned stream,
Which was just like a sort of insurance policy,
Like the mark set upon Cain the murderer.

Or perhaps I was once a rainbow,
Like the rainbow that was the sign of the agreement
(As written in the book of Genesis),
That was made then
Between Noah and his sons and heaven,
So that there should never be another great flood
To destroy life again.

The Early-Arisen Dead Peoples

If the army of Sennacherib, King of Assyria, threatening to
conquer Jerusalem, after it did
"Come up against all the fenced cities of Judah and took them"
It was written in the Bible that *"the angel of the Lord went out
and smote the assyrians...
and when they arose early in the morning,
Behold, they were all dead."*...

And if this happened, as is described in the Bible,
That the corpses saw themselves dead–
It is no wonder that on the painless death
Of the old Victoria, Queen of Britain, it was said:
"At night she went early to bed
And early in the morning
She arose completely dead".

---

* The Second Book of Kings: Chapter 18, verse 13;

Poems on Life, Love and Death

Let Us Start from the Beginning

What is love, or happiness, or sadness?
As we know very well
That these and other powerful feelings
Can shake us like ships tossed at sea,
That these stem from the intricate activities
Among the nerve cells of our brains,
And as we know very well
That the creation of these feelings
Sometimes demand that old patterns be broken,

And as we are striving now
To redesign our own lives,
We should immediately
Rebuilt our old love
From the very beginning
By guiding ourselves to do
These complex actions -
As we know that it is possible,
That it is now within reach.

So let us start now from the beginning
By changing the natural bonds of love,

By changing the language spoken
Between your eyes and my brain
That would decipher their rays of light,
By constructing new sensations
Formed at my fingertips
As they touch
Your blessed skin.

There Is an Instant

There is an instant
Of stolen happiness,
Of overwhelming longing,
Tasting like Ambrosia,
Sweeter than apricot -
Instantaneously.

There is a wind
With a screech bursting in a roar
Of a distant thunderstorm.
And a close murmur passing
Through the green woodland–
Like the wind.

There is rain
Falling on the garden lawn.
Then, suddenly, all at once
A shock of gentle tenderness
Is there with a song of gratitude
For the rain.

There is summer
With its twilight sun
Setting orderly into
A rising haze

In the distant horizon -
In the summer.

There is darkness
As of a dry root
Awaiting to be quenched
By a necromancer,
Who reveals the spirit of poetry
In the darkness.

There is a child
Out of a galloping quiver
And the sweetest blaze
From a craving womb
With ultimate pleasure -
There is a child.

A Different, Other Life

You now know this well:
There is another, different life
That you can also live.
But for that, you must change.
Otherwise you will go backwards
Like the crab at the seaside,
Or else, your end will be bitter and swift;
But, for some reason, you are haunted,
Always daunted,
And the mountains lie ahead clearly
Ever silent and alienated.

A Wind Always Blows

A wind always blows on the island of Madagascar,
A north westerly, stormy wind.
And tropical showers, that fell yesterday in Antananarivo,
Between the gneiss and granite mountains,
Are falling now in the port city of Toamasina on the east coast.

And he who is tired from the day's difficulties
Should perhaps sit down,
And he who is already sitting down
Should lie down;
And he who is lying down now– should sleep,
For he who sleeps here now
May have nightmares
About the ancient revolution
Of breaking away
From the large mass of
The African continent;
Or maybe, amid the noises of the night,
He interprets the sound of bats,
Out hunting frogs
In the equatorial rain forest;
And maybe he also sees the hues
Of the stripy raindrops;
And maybe he also touches the great compassion
Felt in all the places

We were before we were created
And where we shall return – after we cease to be.

Come out, Come out, Bloody Fly

Following the relentless wars in our area; And following Shimei, son of Gera, who cursed King David: *"Come out, come out, thou bloody man".*

(2 SAMUEL, 16:7)

Come out, come out, Tsetse fly
Come and bite till blood trickles, drips
Implant a parasite that would love
To settle under man's skin.

Come out, come out, Tsetse fly,
Bite and drink blood, and
Implant a parasite
Casting a deathly sleep on man.

Come out, come out, you bloody fly
And be the false god, Baalzebub*
You'll be worshipped by the tribes
And offer human sacrifice.

---

* Literally – 'Lord of the flies' and also the name of Canaanite idol

Here's a Man Who Was Born into Wars

(Following 10 wars and battles, defend the State of Israel in its 67 years)

Here's a man who was born in a sandy land,
Whose parents wished he could do what he can
To realize dreams, but he was destined for
Battle. Here's a man who was born into wars.

All his life he tried, in vain, to hope,
To find solutions, or a way to cope;
He had his son, who looked just like him,
But learned that he too was destined for wars.

Here's a man who was born into wars and strife
Despite the opposition of his parents and wife
Who wonder whether his son, who's so good
Will be destined for wars too.

And his son is trying to map out his life
In this land, which grew in the sands
But turned dreams to shattered hopes
For his son too was born into wars.

What is the Motive?

I have known quite a few people
Who have passed through many countries,
From one end of the world to the other,
And now they are people
Who have passed on from this world,
Humans who have gone to their other world
And none of them has returned to tell,
To tell me: is it really
The world of truth there,
Or is it just a different, celestial sphere?

I have known many people in this world
Who are now gone,
And no longer can I ask them
What motivated them to travel the world
And what was the drug that kept them going;
It is doubtful that it was just destiny,
It is more likely that it was
An early genetic order.

Life's Brownian Motion

Like the molecules of gas or liquid
Which move quickly, in all directions,
Without any order,
And on their way,
They crash and change
Their paths ceaselessly;
– So too, in life
This rush
The crashing, and lack of order
Create a sort of dynamic equilibrium
Which is termed, in natural sciences,
The Brownian motion.

Just like the molecules,
So does life too
Constantly move, without any order;
Small movements, crashes,
Changes of direction, scattering,
Immediately they are not here
And they are still not there.
Thus, life is in between
And here is, in the meanwhile,
An intermediary stage.

And that is all, for now
For that is life as of now,
Which has just left the womb
And has almost reached its end
In a sort of wild dance, up and down
To the rhythm of Brownian motion
Which is both not a little
And almost nothing, for now.

All Alone

All animals, each and every one
Born alone – will also die alone:
They came into this world on their own,
They will leave this world alone.

And all that happens in between,
And all that is called by them life
Is mostly a collection of pointless things,
Which, in hindsight, after the end of their lives and actions,
Almost no one will be remembered in the following generations,
Even if their names became famous.

Thus, in life, as it happens
There are many acts of passion,
Such as love-making
Where men try constantly
From maturity till their death,
To return to their mother's womb
Through another woman's pipes.
And so they flow to her

Like *"the rivers run into the sea*
Yet the sea is not full",
And thus, they leave this world
Having fulfilled only half of their desires.

And as for the women
In those acts of love
They eagerly take the men's vitality
To fertilize ovules, get pregnant and give birth.
Sometimes they still take the strength from the men
Which is of no value, like the foam on the waves in the sea,

Like the sea, which even at high tide, is never full,
And so too in other areas –
Things happen over the years
Which seem important, maybe even grand,
They all do not matter at all, in hindsight
In the eyes of those born in the next generations.

Because all sons and daughters of Adam
Are born alone,
Each one of them - on their own
And so too they all die alone.

The Autumn of Our Life

Volcanic ashes are resting for millions of years,
Scattered on our dry fields;
Should migrant birds land there for a moment,
They would take-off immediately
As if fleeing from disaster.

Is it any wonder?
Since these are the charred fields of our childhood,
Bisected by dry footpaths
From which dust rose upon our adulthood
While we gathered and piled up heaps of straw
And lit them to warm up our aging selves –
Right now, in the autumn of our life,
As we move towards the eternal winter nights.

Biography

Nobody asked him what happened
When he cried out at his birth.
Nobody is asking him
What he thinks today.
Nobody will ask him
When he will shut up and pass away.

Because his life is a state
Without a course or calling;
Because his life is but a temporary incident
That offers no cause for celebration,
And at the end he will be entitled to a funeral,
Which, too, is yet another show.
Except, the main character
Is there no more.

And those attending his burial
Will be like a few subscribers
That the deceased picked up incidentally
Walking in the tracks of his life.

About Life, Old Age and its End

a. Introductory Poem

As of today, scientists teach and define,
In their own, short and concise lingo
The nature and identity of life
(Overlooking its quality), as follows:
Life is a collection of traits and features
Of all beings, plants and creatures
Breathing and feeding on various substances,
And then growing and reproducing,
Moving internal organs
And moving externally;
And all this, within their time frame
Between their formation, their old age
And their end – in their death.

b. Confession of Eli, High Priest of Shiloh

"Now Eli was very old"

(I SAMUEL 2:22).

I am already lying in the temple of God in Shiloh
And God's candle is still burning within me,
And the streams of my life flowed long ago,
And they still flow to the sea,
But the sea is not full.
And all things in me are weary:

My heart still beats,
And my lungs breathe in mountain air,
But the streams of my life are going, though slowly,
And diminishing.
And my brain's abilities are decreasing:
I can barely talk any more,
I can hardly see any more,
And listening is very difficult.
And if I still have memories from my early days,
I barely remember anything from the last few days.
And who will remember me – after I am gone?

Confession of the Old Man

Life has an expiry date,
But mine, unfortunately,
Is unknown to me,
For it was not written
On my forehead on my birthday.

Meanwhile, I feel
That my days are running out,
Just like *"all the rivers run into the sea;*
Yet the sea is not full", as written in Ecclesiastes.
Thus my sea is also lifeless,
For it is the Dead Sea.

And as is written in Ecclesiastes
"All things are full of labour"
– So too is my life now:
I do not walk well,
I talk slowly,
I hear a little,
I can only see
Shadows in the background.
And my memory really deceives me,
For things from the past I remember well
But I do not recall at all what I did a moment ago.

But now I would like everyone to know
That there is still a nice old man like me in the world
But, who will remember me after I am gone?

Oblivion

I was not winning any prize,
Nor taken by surprise,
Rather, grasped by a force
I could not resist,
Abducted unwillingly to assist
My forth-coming inevitable fate
– To fall, to sink, on this date
Into oblivion.

Why then, do I wonder
That already now I'm forsaken,
Derelict and smitten
By a dark night, with no morrow,
And by my great sorrow?

Instructions for the Messenger

Go and meet my angel of death.
He is probably disguised as someone else:

He is wearing a striped nightshirt
Made of flax, and his black beard
May have the sawdust of my damp summers stuck to it;
My finest wandering yearnings must
Have been carefully tied to his belt.
Glance downwards and scan –
Whether he wears tilted shoes on his feet
From the use of another man.

Ask how he is, do not be sad!
Whistle the rhythm of my heart's tune to him,
Give him the key to the riddle of my ending life.
Compose my grief in a ballad
Over the missing solutions in the equation
Of my life, full of unknowns.
Apologize for bothering him so early.
Say it is the fault of the giants
(Those sons of God Who came down
to the daughters of Adam;
To be with women, in the flesh).

Say, that I will not be able to live much longer because of them,

Be very old like the men of ancient times,
Some of whom lived for hundreds of years
Of sadness on earth.

So, go and find my angel of death,
And tell him all these things,
– As he looks
Like he is strolling and expecting
Me to call him.

Now, in a Night of Disappointment

Now
When the quiet is taut like a washing line
And your bleary eyes hang off the ceiling,
– In vain will your eyes long
In the middle of the night to close your blinds over me,
Becouse Your running, black pupils,
Chasing the crumbs of light.

Now
All your white memories
Rise from you, like after a bath,
Leaving you right now
To demand an apology from a disappointing night
For disrupting, for drying up your
Sweet streams of dreams, golden dreams.

Now
You listen alone to the sound of your blood
Flowing inside, wandering to and fro
In the usual channels;
You remain listening to the rustles of dawn,
On the prowl for the drops of dew on the grass.

Now
You're already

Listening to the whisper
Of the crashing embers of the sun
Somewhere in the East, which will soon bring
The whole world out to the festival of fire.

Amazement

"They shall be amazed one at another."

(ISAIAH 13:8).

There is nothing more amazing
Than the fleeting time, so surprising
From the moment of creation to now,
As that time lingers
To offer some help and advice
To a man on his way to Hades.

There's nothing more wonderful
Than those sparkling stars in the sky,
Whose light travels speedily to us
From thousands of light years away,
And now they exist no more:
They have already become the darkest black holes.

There is nothing more misleading
Than the glass that seems empty,
For it is full to the brim
With matter unseen,
With transparent air, with no flavour, smell or colour,
Which surrounds all living creatures in nature.

There is nothing more curious, indeed,
Than the one Lord who gives heed
To our prayers and blessings,
 - But He speaks not to us
As we approach crises and dangers.

Of Three and Four

"There be three things which are too wonderful for me, yea,
Four which I know not:
The way of an eagle in the air; the way of a serpent upon a rock;
The way of a ship in the midst of the sea;
And the way of a man with a maid."

(PROVERBS, 30: 18-19)

If the eagle glides in the sky,
It glides in the sky, the eagle;
It glides and glides in the sky
In a journey wondrous and high.

The serpent consumes earth
It consumes earth, the snake;
It consumes and consumed
And I wonder how even, with mirth.

A ship that sinks in the sea,
In the sea, a ship will sink,
Far away in the sea,
And I here will not know, will not see;

When a man 'knows' a young woman,
He 'knows' a young woman, this man;
He sleeps with her in bed,

And I think of that in my head.

For these three are too wonderful for me
The fourth, which I know not,
Don't rest, and do not smile my soul,
Before I think things through;
For only then, my soul,
Will you rest again.

The Decree on the Life of Man

Man's fate is sealed irreversibly,
So ruled the Lord and also said so clearly
To the first man who sinned and hid:
"For dust thou art and unto dust shalt thou return."
That is the decree on life, the fate of a human being,
And this is the order of events before his death:
A bud in his mother's womb,
His birth while screaming to open his lungs,
His childhood in the wonder of his discoveries,
His youth amid his uncertainties,
His young adulthood in his rebelliousness,
His adulthood in the flow of thoughts,
His old age captive to his anxieties,
His last years in his alienation,
And his ending in death.

This is the order of events in the decree on the life of man
In the physical world, which was created by God,
As death ambushes and trims man's life
And finally signs it off too.

Embraces

Between the poems
Embraced are
The alphabet letters.

Between the rivers' arms
Embraced are
The lands in the deltas.

Between the mothers' arms
Embraced are
The suckling babies.

Between the widows' arms
Embraced are
The dead husbands gone suddenly.

Between the closed tight lips
Embraced are
The cries of horror towards heaven.

Woman's Tears

(For the International Women's Day – 3/8/2008)

"Refrain thy voice from weeping,
And thine eyes from tears.
For thy work shall be rewarded..."

(JEREMIAH 31:16)

Refrain your voice from weeping, don't you cry again
Even if I am going today astray;

Don't you cry now, nor shiver, nor fear
Even if I am falling into a trap or pit;

Don't you cry, don't you weep,
Keep the salty tears out of your cheeks.

And if a slice of bread leads a man astray,
Then a drop of your salty tear may carry him to a grave.

But if quietly you are now weeping,
I shall lick shivering a tear after a tear,

'Cause each of your tears purifies
My sins, and atones my bitter fate.

No More, But

"And he said, Thy name shall be called no more Jacob, but Israel:
for as a prince hast thou power with God and with men, and
hast prevailed."

(GENESIS, 32:28)

Not Enoch, the eldest son Of Cain
 The murderer and tiller of the land
– But his distant cousin, the righteous Enoch, son of Jared
Who may have become an angel, as he *"walked with God and*
disappeared, for God took him."

Not Noah, son of Lamech, and his family
Who sailed in the ark on the seas
In the terrible flood, which lasted
Forty nights and days;
And not the Greek Deucalion, son of Prometheus,
Who also stayed in his own ark for nine days and nights
With his wife Pyrrha,
– But Utnapishtim, hero of the Babylonian story of the flood,
Only he did gain eternal life, like the Gods.

Not all liquids lose their volume after they are cooled and
become solids
But only water, which turns into ice when frozen,
Which has much greater volume than liquid.

In all the fundamental chemical elements
There is no liquid crystalline iodine,
For when it is heated, it immediately become gaseous iodine
Without the liquid state.

"Stand in Thy Lot at the End of the Days"*

"In the day ye eat thereof," whispered the snake to Eve,
"Ye shall be as gods, knowing good and evil."**
And perhaps the snake whispered this to Eve too:
"But till the end of your days you shall not know
Which is the day you die"
And so said the old men of
Mycenae to King Agamemnon:***
"Don't dwell on the end of your future,
Await its arrival."
"Stand in thy lot at the end of the days," said the prophet Daniel,
"For the living know that they will die"****
Said Ecclesiastes.

For life was given to you as a gift to be preserved,
Sometimes you shall love it, and sometimes you shall hate it
(As mentioned in Proverbs *"...he that hateth gifts shall live."*)*****
But you shan't know your fate in advance
Nor when your end will come.

---

*   Daniel 12:13
**   Genesis 3:5
***   Aeschylus, the play Agamemnon
****   Ecclesiastes 15:27
*****   Proverbs 15:27

And apart from Jephthah's daughter
Who knew just when she would be sacrificed:
Two months after she would weep in the mountains
over her virginity.
And apart from Cassandra, the princess prophet
Who knew in advance of the destruction of her city,
Troy, and even announced her death before she was killed
(Though no one believed her or her prophecy).

And apart from a few other men, women and prophets like her,
– Humans do not know for certain when their end will come.
And that is the unknown which gives them hope
And strengthens them, helping them to cope.

My Past Now Comes Before Me

My personal future is getting shorter
So much so, that it has almost no shadow
On a hot summer's day, full of sun,
Or else it has just a small one
In the daylight of a cold winter's day.

My future no longer comes before me,
It is my past which comes before me.
Who told me that I would go far in my days
If I stayed close by always?

Those who told me so are the same
As the ravens told to Elijah the prophet, "go on";
Or has done the big fish which
Swallow Jonah and ejected him.

If indeed you too will never know
How far you will go.

I Didn't Know My Flaming Soul

When I first saw you from afar,
I saw you – but did not notice the purity of your beauty.
When I first heard you from afar
I heard but did not listen to the beat of my trembling heart.
But when you approached me – I was astounded.

And like Jacob, who first met Rachel at the Well,
When she approached him, leading her father's sheep herd,
– I also felt the aroma of your delicious scent;
And I, like him, kissed you and cried,
As I did not know my flaming soul of fire
Due to love,
Love alone.

"He That Doth Keep His Soul, Shall Be Far From Them"

(PROVERBS 22:5)

The most despised joy is rejoicing in another's failure;
The most mistaken personal relief
Is sexual gratification by a single person;
The least wisdom
Is the wisdom after the event;
And the most foolish love there is, ever since time began,
Is self-adoration.

But we all do these throughout our lives
And sin thoughtlessly in these things,
Because without meaning to, and only occasionally,
We also rejoice in another's failure,
And satisfy ourselves by ourselves,
And have retrospective wisdom,
And adore ourselves.
And this is all without us noticing it,
"Thus He that doth keep his soul shall be far from them".

Only The Angels

I write sometimes sad poems
That music may be for them lovely.

I execute sometimes dark deeds
That silence must be for them lovely.

I love to love sometimes in the mornings,
For the nights are lovely, but weary.

I am surprised once again by events
Where I am expressive and angry.

I weep much in secret
And only the angels see me.

A Poem of Light

For Deborah the prophetess that *"Her candle goeth not out by night."*

(PROVERBS, 31:18)

The candle light shines in your eyes
In an emerald green;
It is the candle-light chasing you
With the distant wind;
It is like the light of a child's new day,
A reason to celebrate;
It is like the light in the doe's eyes
As she sees her mate;
It is like the light of the north star
Showing the way to those lost;
It is like a guitar
Which never stops
Playing a pleasant tune.

And so, this light seeks you
And a poem of light reaches you.
It is a poem of light,
Yes, it is a poem about a unique pure light.

The Journey South

We left no fingerprints on the pure white paper,
Which tolerates everything.
We did not leave any footprints in the dust of history,
Which does not always return, but always remembers,
Only time has long since left its mark on our faces and bodies;
Therefore we now leave the baggage of our past
And set off on the journey as free people,
As we head out the south
(As we know not what evil is hidden in the North);
With just a hope to make our hearts beat,
 - That we may be happy there in the twilight of our days.

Don't Look Back

Don't look back,
What was done cannot be undone.
Don't look back,
The past is occasionally sad and black.
Don't look back,
On the contrary, enjoy life's feast:
Drink it up in large gulps and eat it up heartily.

Ladies, don't look back
Lest you become very salty,
Like Lot's wife.
Friends, don't look back,
Like Orpheus who did not control his urge
To look back to see his loved wife Eurydice,
Lest what your soul longs for shall be lost there
Lest you, too, shall inherit hell.

Don't look back
And don't get too brave,
But live very much here and now
Before you are taken to the grave.
For this is the real life
And now, there is nothing else but the moment
And only death is the threshold to its end.

The Stream Returned to the Spring

a.

The stream to the spring did return,
The spring went back to the groundwater, in turn;
The rain returned to the cloud, you see
And the cloud suddenly went back to the sea.

b.

The chick returned to the egg,
And the egg – into the hen;
The bread turned into flour again,
And the flour – into a grain.

c.

A man returned to his infancy,
A flute returned to the tree trunk;
The fish in the net returned to the sea,
The match got its fire back.

d.

The future has become the past,
The melody has returned to the piano;

Words have returned to the paper, at last
The poem has returned to the poet, oh.

e.

The rain to the cloud has returned
The egg – to the hen;
Grass has gone back to its roots,
The sea has become a whirlpool again.

f.

The arrow has returned to the bow,
The bow is a tree again now;
Light has become darkness,
Like a movie which has been
Screened in reverse.

"There Is No Light in the Words Said"

"If they speak not according to this word, it is because there is no light in them."

(ISAIAH 8:20)

"There is no light in the words said."
– Thus said the president in denial
To those present at the press conference
And to all the people – via the wireless.

Which is very strange, since if there is no light
 - The sun will not shine any more,
And there will be no more daylight,
And the earth will always be dark
(Just like once there was just darkness
over the surface of the deep);
And the plants will not produce the three major food groups,
And so vegetarian animals will not eat them any more;
And their predators – will not have their meat;
And human beings, who eat both meat and plants,
Will no longer sun bathe on the beach.

But there are many of them
Who expect the first light,
Which will relieve them of nightmares in the dark of night,
And when it comes, they will burn incense in appreciation
In the temple of daylight.

For the Soaring Spirits

For the soaring spirits, who aim high without any hesitation
– Awaits Asmodeus*.
just as what happened to Bellerophon
Who flew high, then fell off Pegasus, his winged horse,
Who was described by Pindar, the greatest
poet of ancient Greece,
A long time ago, more than two thousand five hundred years ago:

"I will search every day for the joy
And so, get older with a peaceful soul.
I will complete my days as it was destined
For we shall all die in any case...

But for the man who aspired and flew
To the home of the almighty God,
Awaited only a bitter end
At the edge of joy,
Which was beyond all measure."

---

* King of demons in Jewish demonology.

Love is Like the Legendary Sphinx

They tell me that love is
Like the legendary Sphinx,
Which swallowed into it
Those who had not solved its riddle.
And to those who had solved only part of it,
The sphinx granted only the illusion
As if they had experienced love;
But that was not the real love,
Which is deep and fierce
And mysterious,
But only a poor substitute
Of the love of the flesh,
Which is without any inspiration
And is not love at all.

Future Poems

Sublimination*

Dedicated to Deborah the Prophetess, Judge and Poetess.

Now you are like the castle in Gibraltar
And compared with you, I am just an amateur rhymer;
I am to you like the foam on the waves,
Always crashing to the cliff with the sound of distant drums.

You are like a half-dormant volcano:
At times erupting, at times inactive;
I swore on that in the Book of Ecclesiastes
For I live beside a mountain, in a house made of basalt.

You are like the Cape of Good Hope, protruding out to sea,
You are vast, high, a wonderful sight to see;
So much so, that I now choke in the atmosphere
Like a gaping fish, swept up on to the beach.

You are so noble and high, forever,
And when I just try to come to you
I'm like crystalline iodine that heats up immediately
And evaporates – turns to gas – I completely disappear.

---

* Sublimation - the transition of a substance directly from the solid to
the gas phase without passing through the intermediate liquid phase.

The Place of the Future

"The future is no longer what it used to be"

(A. Eban)

They say the past is a familiar place
To which many are willing to testify,
But of the future they fear to speak,
For it is a strange and scary domain,
As no one has been there before;
And perhaps there, more than anywhere else,
It is all empty, or bare land full of void,
A worthless place, just desolation.

And although all our hopes stream there,
Like all the waters gathered unto one place,
By God's command in the Book of Genesis,
Which He then called "Seas",
After *"Earth"* appeared as *"the dry land"*
Thus becoming the place of "the beginning",

The distance from which, all the way to us,
Is the value*, definite and unique,
Known as "Past",
That also used to be called "Future" in the past
– To be as long as it could last.

---

* As defined in mathematics: "The absolute value of a number is the distance of that number from the inception."

The Day of Tomorrow

"Boast not thyself of tomorrow,
for thou knowest not what a day may bring forth."

(PROVERBS 27:1)

"The king of today will fall tomorrow"

(BEN-SIRA, CHAPTER X, 10. - 180 YEARS B.C.)

Although we know already
That the tomorrow of yesterday
Is in fact today;
That out of the cocoon of this day
Will break out the butterfly of tomorrow
(And there is no need of magic spell
To inspire its spirit of life),
– Thus like the tadpole that does not know
That it will become a frog tomorrow,
– So neither we know
What will be the acts of tomorrow:
Shall we live on or die ?

But we do know for certain
That tomorrow is another day,
And how much we don't know
What this day may bring forth.

The Twenty First Century

Currently
The olive tree
Still has such green leaves,
And it always has a deceptive fall
Because it is still green as it was before.

But what will happen to the tree and its colour
In a dozen years or so?
Who beside us now will assure
Us that anything will remain of
This very green tree
Apart from space, murky with nothingness?

And perhaps then would the poet ask,
If he would still live and not die:
Was the olive tree here?
Maybe there was nothing there,
Just emptiness?

Progress

(A futuristic poem, written in 1977)

By the year 2027,
The baby's sex and other details
Such as hair colour,
And whether he will be tall or short,
Will be pre-determined.
And then, he will be implanted in his mother's womb
In an ovule, which will be fertilized in vitro.

When he reaches adolescence,
Factories will produce babies
Without any human touch;
And half of humanity will slip into a deep winter's sleep
(And in any case, there will be fewer mouths to feed with
food and water),
The other half will have sharper cognitive abilities
(And in any case, fewer hearts needing love).

Then there will also be a significant change
in human personality:
Humanity will recover from diseases,
And menopause will also be cancelled,
And youth's potency will be extended,
And body organs will be restored,

There will be supervision over ageing,
And the essence of memory will be injected,
And the last frontier of death will be pushed further away.

And then, when he is already middle aged
He will stand and ask, in a rather loud voice:
Where will we go from here
And what else should we expect,
And when will all this – end?

The Fate of Our Great - Grandchildren

"Those who sit in the sty of contentment, Meaning death".
(T.S. ELLIOT, MARINA).

The fate of our great-grandchildren
Who will be born to live
In a world after our time,
– Will they survive then because of our crimes?

It is true, there are many species of plants
And almost another billion hectares of woodland;
There are many kinds of animals on the land
And lots of fish and sea-dwelling creatures.

Deep in the earth, there are natural resources
and quarried substances,
And we have culture, delightful treasures, hi-tech and sciences;
But there are now (in 2015) already seven-and-a-half
billion people in the world,
Who will multiply, reproduce and increase in number
in another fifty years;

They will spread throughout the land and devour its precious
plants and food, like locusts.
They will diminish its resources and pollute its surroundings.
They will disturb its climates and dry up its water resources

– till there is wilderness,
And – in fifty years' time they will wipe out whatever exists...

When nothing will remain
To feed them on earth because of us,
All our great-grandchildren will not be able to live in our
world any more, alas!

But while there is still time,
And we are still alive , the still small voice
Commands us to find some way out,
Some formula which will use what we still have
So that there should be more
Than the surviving remnants
For our great-grandchildren too.

The Crying Female Asses

When the fire broke out in the ancient forest, the virgin forest,
Where they grazed and weeded damaging weeds such as
Bermuda grass,
- The female asses burst out braying bitterly, as a chorus.

They cried more than Kish's female asses cried
when they got lost in the forest,
And Saul, his son, searched for them but could not find them;
(though he tried in earnest).
They even cried more than Balaam's female ass
(Who opened her mouth to speak like a lass
When she saw, even before her master set his eyes
Upon the angel with his sword drawn).
She cried bitterly after she was hit
By him with a stick three times:
As suddenly the path she quit
And pressed his foot to the wall
And under him she decided to stubbornly sit.

Why did the female asses cry during the fire in the forest?
And with them, so did all the mammals and the hoofed animals?
Because even though they did not resemble God
They all have, no doubt, a sensitive soul,
As they have feelings and a consciousness, on the whole
So that if they could now speak like humans

They would surely ask in their inner circle:
What evil did we do to humans in this world, what actions?
How did we sin, so that instead of finding us
— The atmosphere, full of contaminating gases was found,
Which make the world so hot
And will burn our forest and all there is?

The Waters Are Still Hoping

Since it was said:
"Let the waters under the heaven be gathered"
— The waters still gather quickly
And flows- runs in streams to the sea;
And still, the sea is not full,
And still, the sea needs more.

Since it was said –
The streams have flowed to the sea,
But the sea is not complete, ever since then and still today,
As the sea still needs more, and the sea is already tired now;
And the waters, just like they did then, still gather to it.

And they gathered and hope tirelessly,
Still hoping entirely to fill it completely.